Bb TENOR SAXOPHONE

CONCERT FAVORITES

Volume 1

Band Arrangements Correlated wit...
Essential Elements Band Method Boo...

ISBN 978-0-634-05206-4

HAL•LEONARD®

7777 W. BLUEMOUND RD. P.O. BOX 13819 MILWAUKEE, WI 53213

00860126

LET'S ROCK!

Bb TENOR SAXOPHONE

MICHAEL SWEENEY (ASCAP)

00860126

MAJESTIC MARCH

B♭ TENOR SAXOPHONE

By PAUL LAVENDER

00860126

MICKEY MOUSE MARCH
(From Walt Disney's "THE MICKEY MOUSE CLUB")

Bb TENOR SAXOPHONE

Words and Music by **JIMMIE DODD**
Arranged by **MICHAEL SWEENEY**

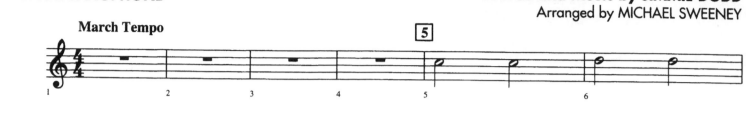

POWER ROCK
(We Will Rock You • Another One Bites The Dust)

Bb TENOR SAXOPHONE

Arranged by MICHAEL SWEENEY

00860126

WHEN THE SAINTS GO MARCHING IN

Words by KATHERINE E. PURVIS
Music by JAMES M. BLACK
Arranged by JOHN HIGGINS

B♭ TENOR SAXOPHONE

March Style

FARANDOLE
(From "L'Arlésienne")

Bb TENOR SAXOPHONE

GEORGES BIZET
Arranged by MICHAEL SWEENEY (ASCAP)

00860126

JUS' PLAIN BLUES

Bb TENOR SAXOPHONE

MICHAEL SWEENEY (ASCAP)

From the Paramount and Twentieth Century Fox Motion Picture TITANIC

MY HEART WILL GO ON
(Love Theme From 'Titanic')

Music by JAMES HORNER
Lyric by WILL JENNINGS
Arranged by PAUL LAVENDER

B♭ TENOR SAXOPHONE

00860126

From THE MUPPET MOVIE

THE RAINBOW CONNECTION

Words and Music by PAUL WILLIAMS
and KENNITH L. ASCHER
Arranged by PAUL LAVENDER

Bb TENOR SAXOPHONE

00860126

SUPERCALIFRAGILISTICEXPIALIDOCIOUS

Words and Music by
RICHARD M. SHERMAN and **ROBERT B. SHERMAN**
Arranged by MICHAEL SWEENEY

Bb TENOR SAXOPHONE

(From "THE SOUND OF MUSIC")
DO-RE-MI

Bb TENOR SAXOPHONE

Lyrics by OSCAR HAMMERSTEIN II
Music by RICHARD RODGERS
Arranged by PAUL LAVENDER

DRUMS OF CORONA

B♭ TENOR SAXOPHONE

MICHAEL SWEENEY (ASCAP)

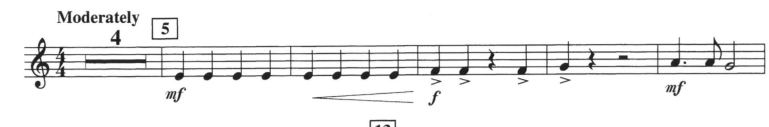

LAREDO
(Concert March)

Bb TENOR SAXOPHONE

JOHN HIGGINS

Allegro

POMP AND CIRCUMSTANCE
March No. 1

B♭ TENOR SAXOPHONE

By EDWARD ELGAR
Arranged by MICHAEL SWEENEY

Majestically

1. Optional repeat to measure 5

2. Optional repeat to measure 29

3.

STRATFORD MARCH

Bb TENOR SAXOPHONE

JOHN HIGGINS (ASCAP)

00860126